THE BROKEN MASTERPIECE
Adoption Perspectives

THE BROKEN MASTERPIECE
Adoption Perspectives

SCOT BOWLSBY and NOAH WITH
XULON PRESS ELITE

Xulon Press Elite
2301 Lucien Way #415
Maitland, FL 32751
407.339.4217
www.xulonpress.com

© 2020 by Scot Bowlsby and Noah With

All rights reserved solely by the author. The author guarantees all contents are original and do not infringe upon the legal rights of any other person or work. No part of this book may be reproduced in any form without the permission of the author. The views expressed in this book are not necessarily those of the publisher.

Unless otherwise indicated, Scripture quotations taken from the New King James Version (NKJV). Copyright © 1982 by Thomas Nelson, Inc. Used by permission. All rights reserved.

Scriptures marked (AMPC) are taken from the Amplified Bible, Classic Edition Copyright © 1954, 1958, 1962, 1964, 1965, 1987 by The Lockman Foundation. All rights reserved.

Scripture quotations taken from the Holy Bible, New Living Translation (NLT). Copyright ©1996, 2004, 2007 by Tyndale House Foundation. Used by permission of Tyndale House Publishers, Inc.

Paperback ISBN-13: 978-1-6322-1285-6
Ebook ISBN-13: 978-1-6322-1286-3

Dedication

This book is dedicated to our parents—those who cared for us no matter what we did or how we acted. Our parents loved us no matter what. I'm grateful for my parents and grandparents who have since passed. They showed me how to live even though I thought I knew better. Now that they have passed, I realize just how much I loved them and how much they taught me.–Scot

First things first. I love my family and I would not trade them for anything in the world. I love them so much it's not funny. I love them all. I am going to be very honest in this book. I have been really vulnerable. Probably the hardest and most emotional thing I have ever done is to write this book. We lead best when we're vulnerable.

I also want to thank every single person that has helped me walk through the valleys of my life. Thank you for celebrating with me. Thank you to my wonderful amazing parents that have protected and fought for me. Thank you for my brothers; you guys are so awesome!

- Noah

Table of Contents

Dedication v
Introduction ix

Chapter 1–Open and Closed Adoptions 1
Chapter 2–Noah's Story 7
Chapter 3–Scot's Story 19
Chapter 4–Dealing with Adoption Related Issues 31
Chapter 5–Community Comparison Identity 43
Chapter 6–Satan Exists 55

Conclusion–God's Faithfulness 65
Appendix 1–Children Ask Questions 69
Appendix 2–Thirty Things Adolescent Adoptees
Wish They Knew About Their Birthparents
But Often Are Afraid To Ask 77
Appendix 3–Thinking About Adoption: FAQs 81
About the Authors 87

.

Introduction

For we are God's masterpiece. He has created us anew in Christ Jesus, so we can do the good things he planned for us long ago. (Ephesians 2:10 NLT)

I really don't feel like I deserve the life that God has given me. He has directed me to tell my story, but because of God, it's not who I am anymore. Though my past is painful and heart-wrenching, I hope by sharing my life's journey, it will inspire others to overcome the issues surrounding their adoption. Telling my story is not an attempt to try to get pity. This story is about how forgiveness and reconciliation with the people that hurt me have brought me true freedom.

This story is about sharing how having the faith and boldness to know God loves you even when others hurt you can change your life. God sees you in your mess and brokenness and wants you to know He is forming you into His masterpiece. This story is meant to inspire you and then for you to share it with others who need to be encouraged and inspired as well. This story is about victory in Jesus and becoming all that God has called you and me to be in this life.–Noah

Jesus led Noah to share the Good News with me. I began going to church wanting to feel "a part of" something rather than "apart from" things. When I asked Jesus to come into my life, He completely changed me. Now, I feel compelled to write a book sharing our two stories so others may know the power of Jesus.

This is an account of my life living with a closed adoption. My adoptive parents were great and did the best they could at the time. We all change for the good or bad as we journey through this life. I thank Jesus I'm saved and now have Him to help guide me on the path to freedom.–Scot

CHAPTER 1
Open and Closed Adoptions

Decades ago, virtually all adoptions were closed. However, the trend in the United States today is toward open adoptions.

Open Adoption is a form of adoption in which the biological and adoptive families have access to varying degrees of each other's personal information and have an option of contact with one another as the child grows up. In Open Adoptions, adoptive parents may have access to more of their child's medical or social history than Closed Adoptions. Most adoptions today are Open Adoptions.

Open Adoption: Pros and Cons

For both the birth parents and the adoptive parents, the Open Adoption process can remove the mystery from the adoption process and can permit a greater degree of control in the decision-making process. The Open Adoption process also allows adoptive parents to better answer their children's questions about who their birth parents were and why they were adopted. Open Adoptions can also help the child come to terms with being adopted because the child's concerns can be addressed directly by everyone who was involved in the adoption process.

However, there can also be downsides to Open Adoption. Many adoptive parents find the degree of openness to be a threat, fearing that the birth parents will intrude upon their lives after the adoption is completed or even seek to have the child returned to them at a future date. Adoptive parents may worry that the child will be confused over who his or her "real" parents are.[1]

Adoptive parents may prefer the idea of a Closed Adoption because they will not have to worry about a complicated relationship with a birth mother. While a Closed Adoption does eliminate any risk of a rocky relationship, it also eliminates the possibility of a fulfilling, positive relationship with the birth mother. Moreover, birth mothers cannot reclaim their children under any circumstance.[2]

A Closed Adoption means that no contact whatsoever between the birth parents and the adoptive parents and child after the adoption takes place. If adoptive parents have chosen Closed Adoption as a preference, they may feel Closed Adoption allows them to parent without worry that an Open Adoption would confuse their child.

A birth parent may choose to keep an adoption closed because an open adoption would be too difficult emotionally watching someone else raise their child.

Closed Adoption Difficulties for the Child

- Struggles with Low Self-Esteem
- Identity Issues, "Where do I fit in?"
- Difficulty Forming Emotional Attachments

---

[1] https://family.findlaw.com/adoption/open-vs-closed-adoption.html

[2] https://consideringadoption.com/adopting/open-adoption/open-vs-closed-adoption-an-honest-comparison

- A Sense of Grief or Loss
- Lack of Medical or Social History
- No knowledge of where they inherited genetic psychological traits
- No answers about why they were placed for adoption
- Little or no information on the biological family

Questions to Consider When Adopting:

- Why am I adopting?
- What are the circumstances around the adoption?
- What culture/ethnic background are the biological parents? Does it coincide with your beliefs? What effect will it have on the child?
- What are my expectations?
- Is it a birth, toddler, tween, teenager, or special needs adoption?
- With any adoption, the more pre cise medical and emotional background you have available, the more at ease the child will be. The more you know the more you can fill in the child. They will have questions at some point especially if they are different than you.
- Is there any healthcare or hygiene information you can obtain?
- If the child is from another country, medical information may be hard to get.
- When your child asks questions about his heritage, be prepared to go into detail about all the information you can get. Let the information be age-appropriate.
- Do not lie about the adoption. Tell them the truth and again make it age-appropriate.

Questions Adopted Kids May Ask:

- Why was I adopted?
- Where am I from?
- Why didn't my parents want me?
- Why don't I look like you?
- Can I see my real parents? Why not?
- Are my real parents alive or dead?
- Why did you pick me?
- Did you pick me up at the hospital?
- Did you have to pay money for me? Why?
- Was there something wrong with me?
- Is that why my parents didn't want me?
- Was it my fault?
- Why couldn't I do anything about it?
- Will I ever find my parents?
- Why did they leave me?
- Can I ever meet them?
- Do they want to have a relationship with me?
- What are my genetics?

Pause and Reflect...

If You Are Considering Adopting: You can see from reading the descriptions of both Open and Closed Adoptions, there are important questions to ask and consider.

It is also important to review the questions the child you adopt is eventually going to ask you. Take these into consideration when deciding on an Open Or Closed Adoption.

If You Are Considering Putting Your Child Up For Adoption: It is very important that you carefully consider not only the types of adoptions, but also the future you are establishing for your child.

Note: It's important to keep in mind that, while adoption relationships can change, it is more complicated to increase contact than to decrease it. If a birth mother starts with an open relationship and then decides later that she needs distance, she can do this at any time. However, if an adoption is closed and a birth mother wants more contact, then she has to come to an agreement with the adoptive family. Therefore, it is especially important that a birth mother choosing Closed Adoption is sure that it is what she wants.[3]

---

[3] https://consideringadoption.com/adopting/open-adoption/open-vs-closed-adoption-an-honest-comparison

CHAPTER 2

Noah's Story

I was adopted at the age of seven and never knew my birth mom. I did know her name is Andrea. All I know about her is the ugly, messy things I was told about her. It was an open adoption case. When my adopted mom first came into my life, I was confused, lost, yet I knew she loved me. I knew she was there for me.

You rarely hear about a biological mom leaving her kids. Sometimes you do but not really that often. A lot of the time, it's the father that leaves the family not the mother. Even from a natural perspective when you look at animals, it is generally the father that leaves and never returns, but the mom always sticks with them.

I love my adopted mom and always will no matter what. However, growing up I still had a fear of her leaving because I was insecure and did not know who I was. I would react in a negative way. I would beg my adopted mom to tell me stuff that I already knew. I would ask questions to pick on her and get her angry and upset, but I would be the one getting upset. I would push her buttons so much at the most inconvenient times because I just wanted answers. I have always searched for answers. I think we all search for answers, but it may be tougher on adopted children because answers are harder to obtain.

I kept asking questions like, "Was it my fault Andrea left?"

"No," my adopted mom would say. "Noah, it was never your fault. Stop taking the guilt and shame from someone else's bad decisions."

My adopted mom knew what was best for me, but I still struggled a lot. My fear of abandonment didn't just go away. It was a journey I would have to walk through to overcome all of my fears. I would fall asleep in despair at a very young age, though I would still do normal things that kids did like play and have fun.

In second grade, I ran away from home because I wanted to be with my Nana and Papa, but I did not get very far. I had gone down the street with my older brother, but we both got super scared and quickly ran back home. Rightfully, we were grounded for what seemed like forever.

At the end of third grade, I tried to commit suicide because I felt like I did not have enough attention. I got diagnosed with depression, anxiety, and ADHD from a super young age. Our parents never stopped loving us and making sacrifices for us, though. They were trying to do the best they could.

I went to church and did all the good things that Christians are supposed to do. I also got baptized because I felt like it was the right thing to do. I even preached in the back of the car. I said I was going to be a missionary, travel the world, and show people that they are loved from a very young age. I think that was God literally working in my life.

God was speaking to me, but, I just did not know it until later. It was like I was living two separate lives. One was for God and the other was living in loneliness and fear.

I remember going to be tested for depression. I remember the exact car that we drove to take those tests for depression and suicide. The test of my depression and anxiety would forever change me. They put me on medication. What third grader gets diagnosed with depression and anxiety? Looking back at it, I believe it was just a reaction to something I didn't know how to handle. However, I did not know what caused the reaction or how to react.

I do know I hated the fact that my birth mom left me, lied to me, and destroyed things inside of me and my brother. I didn't understand how or why a mother could do that. It didn't make sense. So, in third grade, I was taking medication that would affect my attention and mood. I know why my parents put me on the medication. It was because I ran away and tried to hurt myself. My parents have helped me so much.

Even so, I continued to act out in elementary school and even middle school. I was really just searching for something to sustain me because I desperately wanted to meet my birth mom. I felt like if I met her, things would be better. All of my life this has been a desire in me to meet my birth mother.

We have been going to church my whole life, but I honestly really started to follow God in between ninth and tenth grade. When I was in eighth grade, someone committed suicide and I realized I would need to face my problems and not get stuck in them or that would be me. I needed to push forward to something that made me better.

I still had unanswered questions. My brother Aaron and I sat down and talked to my parents about what was going on. I will never forget that night.

I asked them, "Does Andrea have another kid? Do I have another brother that I don't know about?"

The answer was, "Yes."

The answer filled me with tears. I have never cried so much in one single moment of my life. I did not know how to process that or what I felt. I know it was incredibly hard to handle. It was like the puzzle was not fully solved. I was a ninth-grade high school student. I knew there was a problem, but solving the problem seemed impossible to me. My family loved me then and still do, but they, too, were at a loss of how to help me.

I had started to go to a Bible study in eighth grade, but I just felt so fake. It was almost like I was a fake believer. God still used it though to begin to make a difference in that time of my life. In ninth grade, it felt like my emotions were all wanting to get out. I did not know how to express myself to get them out in a healthy way. I started to heavily watch porn during the summer between eighth and ninth because I did not know who I was or what I was supposed to do with my life.

Then a good friend of mine invited me to go to this Bible study called Catalyst. I still went to church every single week with my parents, but it was time to make my faith my own. I started going to the Bible study group. I began to see community start to form (see chapter 5 for more information on Community Comparison Identity). It made me really jealous at first because it seemed like these people had it all figured out, but truthfully no one does. Every single person struggles.

At that time in my life, I experienced community for the first time, but I still felt insecure and scared that I would be left alone. There was so much fear in me that I would go anywhere and everywhere with my parents just to be sure that they would not leave me, especially my adopted mom. I knew that she would not leave me, but I still had that fear. I still felt alone.

God was present even though I felt like I wasn't present with Him. He put people in my path to help me to become a man instead of the boy I once was. I started talking and connecting more with my grandma. That woman taught me so much about compassion and loving others. She showed me how loving Jesus is and taught me how to be a better person. She taught me a lot.

It wasn't like I did not know **about** Jesus, but I wanted and needed to really **know** Him. I was searching for something that was always there, but I didn't know it. There was like a big huge hole my heart that God is still healing to this day. It just felt like something was missing. The road to resurrection and forgiveness is hard, but worth it.

When I officially accepted Jesus in my heart, my life was far from being good. I took the first step, but then I needed to learn to walk in my new-found faith. If anything, I found growing in faith makes things harder, but it also pushes us to become better people than what we think we are or believe we can become.

My grandma continued to help me grow in my faith. She died right before Thanksgiving and I missed her a lot. I started to realize after my grandma's death that my family is everything. That changed my perspective on a lot of other things in my life as well.

Thoughts About My Birth Mother

During this time, I began to deal with my feelings about my birth mother. I felt like I just needed to say sorry to her. I had always blamed myself. I thought somehow it had to be my fault that she left, but then I realized it couldn't be because I did not do anything wrong. I wasn't even old enough to actually remember anything that happened to this woman. I really don't remember her at all.

I desperately wanted to know that there was good in her somewhere. However, no one would tell me that there was good in her. I believe everyone has a bad side, but I also believe with God it can be turned into good. I believed there was still hope for her no matter what.

People would ask me, "How can you say that? She abandoned you, Noah. How can you reach out to her? She ruined your life?"

I was learning about forgiveness. I not only had to forgive Andrea, I had to forgive me, and my mom that raised me. Forgiving someone does not make it okay or right for what they did. Forgiving means **you** are no longer bound because of what they did. I had to forgive three people. One was my mom that raised me because I definitely think we said both said some hurtful things in the past. I had to forgive her for that. I wanted to be in control using the anger and bitterness that was affecting me so much. Then I had to actually say, "I am sorry for hurting you mom," and ask her to forgive me.

The second person I had to forgive was my birth mom. For a long time, I felt like I had a right to be angry and wondered why I should forgive her when literally my whole life was a lie. She was my birth mom, what mother would just leave not one but two kids with their Dad and runaway? A mom is supposed to be the person that loves you the most and yet my birth mom left. There was just a lot of hurt in that. The things that my birth mom had done had a tight grip on me. I kept asking myself, "When will it just go away? Why can't I move on?" I think my biggest fear was that she was not ever going to change and be a better person. I deeply yearned for my birth mom even though I was hurt and angry for what she had done.

I was holding onto something I could not have controlled. I blamed myself because I felt like that would solve the problem. To forgive, I had to allow myself to be broken and accept what happened to me even though I did not understand it.

When you are hurting like that, it's a slow and steady process to forgive. You start to just get sick of being sick and tired. You don't automatically run to Jesus. You hurt, but Jesus meets you where you're at and where you need it.

I realized to forgive someone I had to release fear and worry. I started to walk and just talk with Jesus about this. He kept speaking to me about it.

He said, "On the cross, I forgave the prisoners that were hanging right beside Me. The prisoners did not say, 'I really need to be forgiven,' but the Father forgave them for their mistakes."

To be forgiven, we must forgive. I remember writing hate letters to my birth mom and then throwing them away. I also remember the first time I ever forgave my birth mom. It wasn't easy because I wanted to hold onto the things that hurt me. I think forgiveness is a lifelong process. We constantly have to work through the process. I am still forgiving her when things come up that cause hurt and fear.

If we really want to take our faith seriously, we have to realize that we are all imperfect people. Once we realize how broken we are, we realize how beautiful our God is. I think in my heart I know my birth mom is forgiven. I am not rooted in her or the mistakes she has made or even what she has done. Forgiveness is not a feeling, it's an act of obedience that we choose with our minds that will eventually change our hearts.

Once we possess the freedom forgiveness gives us, why would we want to still be held captive by the past? I want to walk in freedom. I am deeply rooted in Jesus Christ and what He has done in my life. When we forgive, there is so much freedom that we get to experience. I think that when we forgive others, we realize that we are forever forgiven.

Loving My Birth Mom

Loving the person that hurt you is definitely difficult. Loving the person that left you scarred, bruised, and with wounds that are hard to heal is not easy. I don't just mean saying, "I love you." No, I am not talking about a worldly love to love the person that has done the most damage to me. I am talking about an eternity love. Jesus calls us to love those kinds of people. Jesus died for the people that hurt us, too. He calls us to deeply love even the people that hurt us. That is super hard.

My biggest desire is not for her to know me. If my birth mom gets to know me that would be incredibly amazing. I have imaged meeting her. If I met her, I would just want to know her as a person even if she is bad. However, my biggest desire is that she would know Jesus. If she knows me, I am not going to last forever. I don't know if it's my place yet to share the gospel with her, but it is absolutely my place to show her the gospel through forgiveness and love and then use words if necessary. I think loving her would not be any different from loving the people around me already.

She does not deserve to be loved, but Jesus doesn't want any of us to base our forgiveness on our feelings. Jesus wants us to walk by faith and not by sight. I could say the same thing about myself when it comes to the forgiveness Christ extended to me. I don't deserve anything. I am literally nothing without God. While I was still dead in my sin, Christ shed His blood for me (see Romans 3:23, and 5:8).

She doesn't deserve it, but my heart is to love her. How do I do that? In the Bible, it talks about the first step to loving someone is being patient with them. So, I am going to try to be patient and kind and rely a lot on the Holy Spirit to lead me. If I am supposed to meet her, I will.

Depression, Anxiety, and ADHD

I think I have only told one person other than my parents about my struggles with depression, anxiety, and being diagnosed with ADHD, so bear with me. It's hard to relive this, but I feel someone reading this book needs to hear it.

In third grade, they tested me for depression, anxiety, and ADHD. I was put on pills because I was self-harming. I don't know why I was doing that, but at that age, I don't think my brain could understand what I was trying to process what was going on in my life.

In third grade, they also diagnosed me with writing, reading, and math disabilities. I would have to be in a special room for math, reading, and writing. They said I would always have a hard time in school, especially writing. As the years went by, I still didn't understand these things and they said it was because of a brain development issue. They said it would affect me the rest of my life and that it was part of my genetics. The genetics part is very true as there were similar issues with my dad.

It seemed like I was fighting multiple battles at the same time, but it was really about just one issue—trying to be good enough. There was a constant pressure I put on myself to perform at the highest achievement level to prove I was good enough. I wanted the outcome of the battle to be a victory and I wanted to achieve it all by myself.

I don't know what caused this or why I have this disability, but all throughout school I struggled. I also struggled with asking for help. I did not want help, I wanted to be normal like the rest of my peers. I have always been an anxious test taker. It was probably because I always struggled with math, writing, and reading. I would come home and work on my homework for hours and hours on end and never seem to get anywhere.

So, it turns out what caused the battle in the first place could only be won by a team effort. We want to take charge, but to take charge, first we have to lose. I have lost so many times. Every time I fight against myself, I lose. I was constantly on a battleground that I didn't know if I could ever win.

I remember in my sophomore year of high school, I finally wanted to try and be successful and ask for help. What's crazy about looking back on this is every time I refused help, the teachers relentlessly pursued me to try to help me anyway. I think the most influential teacher I had was Mrs. Shalor. She was my freshman and sophomore year special ed teacher.

She said, "Noah, you have talents other than school. You connect with people and you have a heart for the broken and for the people hurting. When you are helping others, it helps people see the brokenness beyond beauty that they don't see for themselves."

I don't really know what my response was at the time, but it got me thinking, "What are my gifts and talents? How can I see people beyond their brokenness and the beauty for who they are? How can I help people if I am broken myself?"

The answer is, we have a Heavenly Father that wins every battle every single day. It all starts with one step. That one step leads us into our greatest destiny. We have to step out and keep on stepping up. It is a step of faith. We need to want to constantly run to the arms of Jesus. When we run into His arms, we are embraced in the Father's arms of love. We have to learn this and understand that we can go to Him every day and every time we feel an attack coming against us. He even tells us the battle belongs to Him (see 2 Chronicles 20:15).

My Senior Year

So, I have a learning disability. People always doubted me. I had to constantly overcome the anxiety of school. In my senior year, I did just that! I graduated with over sixty college and high school credits. I am in the process of writing this book. People would tell me I can't do it and I will never make it. Even so, I had a choice to either be stuck where I was or let Jesus lead me further into His arms. I choose to push through it. I wanted to be better. I ask Jesus for help and He led to those who could help me achieve above and beyond what I ever thought possible!

What Jesus did for me, He will do for you as well. Your worth is not in academics or your grades. At the end of the day, that is all just a set of numbers. It's not really going to matter when it's all said and done. At the end of the day, school is important, but it's not who you are. You are talented, gifted, and treasured. Jobs and people matter, but they are not who you are. We all are a broken shattered mess. We are literally nothing but dust without Jesus. With Jesus everything changes. You find your value in Him. The world is going to leave you empty every time. Jesus will fill your life every time.

It's been really hard to continue moving forward and it still is some days. However, because of my faith in Jesus, He has made a way where I thought there was no way. My job is to choose Jesus every single day of my life. I also don't want to be satisfied with where I am at with Jesus. I want more. I want to go deeper into the presence of Jesus. My life is not about me. It's all about how Jesus uses me to fulfill the destiny God has placed within me.

The Master builder is always growing and building something. I have prayed for Jesus to take my pride away. I have so much pride and I need to be filled with humility. I want to live in humility, righteousness, and obedience. It is incredibly difficult to do that all the time, especially if I am trying to do it in my own strength.

Jesus never calls us to the easy road, though. If it was easy, we would all be doing it all the time. That's not the case. It's hard to humbly serve others and be okay with not getting recognized for it. It's so easy to be prideful. Dare I say pride is really based on insecurity? It is with me for sure. It is insecurity that I face on a daily basis. Jesus is making me humble by telling me these works I do are not mine. They are to serve Him and others (see Galatians 6:7-10). That totally changes my whole perspective.

You have no idea how very hard it has been for me to do this book. I did not even imagine writing a book two or three years ago. Jesus has called me to do the things that are very difficult for me to do. I constantly struggle with being confident in who Jesus has made me to be. I want to live boldly in humility, so I have to remind myself who Jesus says I am and what my mission is life is all about.

Jesus has continually challenged me to grow and step out and up to help others. This past summer I worked at a Christian youth camp. I will be leaving soon for a year-long Missionary Prep Program. God is so amazing!

Pause and Reflect...

Jesus said, "On the cross, I forgave the prisoners that were hanging right beside Me. The prisoners did not say, 'I really need to be forgiven,' but the Father forgave them for their mistakes."

What does this mean to you and me concerning how we should forgive others?

What did Jesus say about what we need to do to be forgiven in Matthew 6:14-15?

Read Colossians 3:12-14.

What did you learn about forgiving others from this passage of scripture?

Read Romans 3:23 and 5:8.

What did you learn about Jesus' sacrifice for you from these scriptures?

My teacher said, "Noah, you have talents other than school. You connect with people and you have a heart for the broken and for the people hurting. When you are helping others, it helps people see the brokenness beyond beauty that they don't see for themselves."

What talents has God given you that He wants you to use for His kingdom work?

What does Galatians 6:7-10 tell you to do as you use the gifts and talents God has given you?

How did my story in this chapter impact your life?

CHAPTER 3
Scot's Story

Adopted April 26, 1960
Sixteen-year-old mother
Eighteen-year-old father in the US Navy
First memory: Heartbeat changed, yelling, and screaming

My first real memory was watching Kennedy's funeral procession on TV and my adopted mom crying. Dad had left earlier that month after their divorce, so I thought that was why she was crying. I asked who that man was on the TV and she said it was the President.

My adoptive parents were married in 1951 and divorced in 1963. They adopted me in 1960 and then got divorced three years later. My adopted dad always blamed me for the divorce. However, he soon had a girlfriend and married her in 1964. During this time, my dad would come to get me and drop me off with his new wife and then go hunt, fish, and skeet shoot. He liked to hunt turkey, duck, and geese. I told him I didn't like to hunt or fish. It seemed cruel to shoot these fine animals. That was my adopted mom's doing, so he decided not to subject me to going with him.

I have a memory of waking up in the twin bed in my adopted mom's room, scared to death. I tried to scream but couldn't move. The closet door opened and a big black mass came out of the closet growling and hissing. It had glowing red eyes. It stood right over me and growled, "You are mine now." I always felt a different kind of anger after that. When it went back to the closet, I was able to scream. I told my adopted mom what happened, but she didn't believe me. She said it was a nightmare, but I knew that it wasn't.

In 1964, my adopted mom married my adopted dad's divorce attorney. Very weird, I know. It was like revenge for my adopted mom. I wasn't told until I was eighteen the connection, though. They had a daughter in September of 1965. My half-sister Stacie and I grew up together. We were exact opposites, though. She was outgoing and very social. She has always had high self-esteem. I did not. I was socially awkward, did not like to meet anyone, and had very low self-esteem.

My adopted dad and his friends would tease and scare me sometimes until I cried and then he called me names. By kindergarten, I was afraid of everything. I felt different, less than others, and didn't like school. My self-talk was already self-loathing. I felt like I was thrown away by my biological parents. I couldn't please my adopted dad or his wife. I couldn't please my adopted mom's husband either. I was the step-kid who was totally confused with mixed messages from the adults in my life.

My next few years, I was afraid, angry, and hostile. It felt like it wasn't me; like there was another force inside me. I lashed out at everyone and everything. Then I would be as sweet as ever. It seemed I struggled with simple things, but I was very intelligent and could remember facts, history, etc. easily. I would make an instant decision and believe it to be true even when it wasn't.

I was awkward and anti-social. I didn't like meeting people or going to new places. I thought I was a piece of garbage. I reiterated that constantly in my mind. It was keeping me from reaching my true potential. The deceiver had a grasp on me and wouldn't let go. I would try to make jokes and make fun of myself in a derogatory light to cover up the hurt and insecurity I felt at being different.

I had rage. I didn't know where it came from, but it was always there. The older I got, the worse it became. My outbursts would come at the most inopportune times. In grade school, I would pick fights and let them beat me up. I felt I deserved it

I always had questions about my biological parents. The only thing I was told was my biological mother was too sick to care for me and my biological Dad died in the Navy from pneumonia. The reality that I found out later was my biological mom was sixteen and got pregnant by my biological father. He was an opium addict and died of withdrawal symptoms on the ship after an Asian tour. When my biological mother found out her man had died, her parents made her give me up for adoption. My birth dad died six months before I was born. I was adopted at birth.

More anger and self-loathing developed and I became like two people; a Jekyll and Hyde. Sometimes, I would be cordial and other times I would rage. My adopted mom was very involved in the extended family and their ancestry. I always felt different because they all knew their history, but I didn't know mine. That's the main contention I have with closed adoption. You don't know your history and you feel like you don't belong. I seemed to fit in with the family to a point, but I always thought I didn't belong.

Defective

In 1967, at the age of seven, I was molested by a female babysitter who was a family friend. It affected me to the core. The new message planted within me was, "See, you are defective. You are a piece of garbage."

I was raised in the Lutheran Church. I was baptized as an infant and went to confirmation classes, but all I heard was fire and brimstone and you're going to hell. I didn't take it for real.

I struggled from ages seven to twelve and behaved very badly. I was a rage-filled brat. My adopted dad would get me on Saturdays.

He did not go to church. He swore off God. He was mad and angry all the time. He blamed me for his divorce. Three years before he died, he did finally tell me he loved me. We made amends and I had no more rage toward my adopted dad. I did still have anger at everyone outside the family.

In 1964, my adopted dad re-married and they got pregnant and had a miscarriage. In 1969, my half-brother was born. In 1972, my other half-sister was born. I was so much older than them we never connected.

In 1972, at the age of twelve, my rage began to be a part of my daily life. I was so rageful I couldn't do anything positive. I began to smoke cigarettes and tried alcohol. I was doing anything to get away from my feelings of utter despair. During this time, I went to confirmation classes at my adopted mom's insistence. I went through the motions, but I didn't believe what they were saying so it had no impact on my life.

That summer, I tried marijuana for the first time. I was hooked. It was just what I was looking for because it left me numb with no feelings of rage or anything else for that matter. High school was a blur. I got high every day before school. I began drinking regularly and using speed occasionally. I tried LSD and Cannabinols which kept me "tripping" for six straight hours.

In 1976, at the age of sixteen, I drank a pint of Bacardi 151. I was drunker and higher than I had ever been. While riding my bike the eight blocks home, I was hit by a car and broke my femur. I was in traction for a month, but it didn't heal right. Eventually, my right leg would become an inch and a half shorter. I lived with it and walked with a limp until I was forty-five when the VA gave me built-up shoes.

In January of 1977, at the age of seventeen, I went into the delayed entry program for the Army. I wanted to be like my adopted dad and grandpa. I went to take the physical exam, but did not pass the duck crawl because of my femur injury.

They told me to go to see the Air Force recruiter. There I scored the highest they had ever seen for computers. They offered me a computer programming slot in Omaha, two hours from where I lived. However, I wanted to drive trucks in California. God had a plan for me which I did not follow. I got what I wanted and was sent to California. There I got in trouble for being drunk and high. They never got a dirty UA from me because they weren't perfected yet.

I was on active duty for one year and three months. Luckily, the JAG officer assigned to my case got me an honorable discharge with all my benefits. I always felt guilty for only being in a year and three months. That started the shame cycle I stayed stuck in for many years.

I came back home and immediately started drinking and smoking pot. I got two OWIs in two months. By this time, I was a raging alcoholic with rage and anger as my normal disposition.

For the next three years, I partied. I tried college and failed. Then I went to community college and failed. Then I met and began dating a girl. One night in March of 1981, she said it was me or drinking. My exact thought was, "I'll show that bitch, I'll go to AA." I went to my first meeting drunk. I heard them say he won't be back. I went to the same meeting the next night sober. I stayed in AA for eighteen years. I stayed with her and we were married in October of 1983.

My life now consisted of meetings and getting better. I started working in an adolescent substance abuse treatment center. I was active in AA, but ignored my wife. I would leave her at home 4-6 nights a week while I went to AA meetings or functions. For all practical purposes, we were roommates, not husband and wife.

My life took a good turn, but I was still angry, rageful, and shame-filled. Even though I quit drinking and using drugs, my inner self did not change. I began searching for something else to relieve those symptoms.

I took the Substance Abuse Counseling Certificate test. I was the only one at the center that passed the test the first time. I bet my coworkers I would pass and they would not. I did and they didn't. They had college. I didn't. Since I was a Veteran, they gave me the Department of Corrections clients to work with.

My career was going well, but my marriage crumbled. We were unable to have kids. We divorced in 1986.

In 1987, I met my second wife. We were married in 1988. We moved to a small town and I worked at the substance abuse center. Initially, I was working with kids. Then I worked with the Department of Corrections clients that were on probation and parole. I was there for three years. I had a reputation that hardcore cases would get sober. I knew I wasn't doing it on my own, but I didn't have a relationship with Jesus. I just had a vague idea of God and figured He had gifted me and was helping me.

In April of 1988, I enlisted in the Army National Guard. I excelled because I was sober. I was the drug and alcohol liaison for our company. I was in for six years. It took away my guilt for being in so short of a time in the Air Force when I was younger.

In 1990, my first son was born. Thirteen months later, my second son was born. Since my name was baby boy Alloway until my final adoption in 1961, I desperately reached out to all the Alloway's in Omaha searching for information concerning my medical history. I couldn't tell my boys their medical history from my side because I got no response from anyone with that last name.

In 1990, I got a job at the state working in the minimum-security prison as a counselor. I was there for four years. By 1993, I was divorced from my second wife. I quit the job at the prison and drifted for a year before moving back to my home town. I was still sober, but I was still searching for something to fix my deficiencies and make me feel whole and normal.

In 1996, I met my third wife. She was in AA as well. I thought she was the woman that could fix my problems. I went to work for a mortgage company and again excelled. I was soon transferred to Charlotte, North Carolina.

In September of 1998, my negative self-talk and shame for my actions drove me to begin drinking and smoking pot again. I did not like it in Charlotte at all, so after four years, I divorced my third wife and moved back to my home town again. I was so glad to get back.

I was still at the mortgage company. Even though I was using again, I was still excelling at work, but I couldn't live with myself. So, in 1999, I went to the VA for help the first time. They told me to come back when I could control my rage. I told them that was what I was there for.

I quit the mortgage company in 2004. When I left, they hired two people to take over the job I was doing. I had to train both of them before leaving. From there I went to an insurance company. I was out of a job for two hours, but only lasted with the insurance company for six months. That was the last time I worked.

In March of 2004, I met a therapist named Cindy who agreed to meet with me. We had three, hour-long sessions. It was intense! Years later she told me, "I thought you were going to kill me! I had my hand a quarter of an inch from the panic button the whole time."

She told me it would get worse before it got better and in three to five years, "You'll reach the lowest lows you'll ever have."

She was right. Later in 2004, I took forty-five Clozapine. I woke up two hours later. No one takes forty-five Clozapine and lives, but I did. God was not done with me.

Between 2004 and 2011, I was in the Nut House and Domiciliary nine times. The Nut House was never fun. You were in pajamas and had non-slip socks for shoes. They would leave you there from three days to a month depending on your needs. I would usually be in for 2-3 weeks. They would over medicate me so I couldn't get out of hand.

One particular visit, they had to put me in the "quiet room." I was strapped to a cold steel table by my hands, waist, and legs. I was in there for two days. My rage came out and did not leave. After each time at the Nut House, they would send me to the domiciliary for a three-month stay.

In 2006, it hit me again. It was 39 below zero. I got drunk and sat down in a yard and waited to die. God told to get up, so I did. I was taken home by a good Samaritan. I had frostbite and ended up losing four of my fingertips. That got me a three-month trip to the Knoxville VA. I lost forty pounds and was healthier than I had ever been. I smoked for the first two weeks, but quit while I was healing. I went from there to the Veteran's Home for more rehab. I was there for eight months. After I healed, I went back to smoking cigarettes again because I really had not dealt with my core issue.

Tom

In 2004, I met Tom, who became my dearest and closest friend ever. We were both adopted and had PTSD. He was a huge Cubs fan and so was I. We both were "retired," basically dealing with our rage by drinking and smoking pot. Tom was the first person I could tell anything to and not feel like there was any judgment or condemnation. We started going to a PTSD group for men at the VA. We were both doing individual therapy with Cindy and it seemed natural to start a group where we worked with new men coming into the group.

When he was diagnosed with lung cancer, I would pick him up at 8:30 in the morning. While he was in the VA for cancer treatments, I would have two crockpots going at my apartment trying to prepare food he could eat. He gained twenty-four pounds in three weeks under my care. We would eat and then watch three baseball games every day. It's what he wanted to do.

Then the VA found out what I was doing and told me I couldn't take him to my apartment or come to see him at the VA any more even though I was doing better at healing him than they were. In the following week, he lost thirty-five pounds and the will to live.

Tom died of lung cancer in November of 2014. All he wanted to do was make it to Veterans Day, he died two days after that, but he showed me how to live during the time we had together.

Tom and my friend Bob both died of cancer, but these men showed me how to be a "real" man, how to cry, admit fault, be vulnerable, and love.

I filed for a pension for PTSD from the service. They determined that I did have PTSD and they gave me a service-connected partial pension. First it was 30 percent. Over the next few years, it went to 70 percent. In 2014, I was given a Congressional honor for all my work with myself and other veterans. It is The Order of the Teal Cross. It was then I got my full pension.

I was finally able to pay my bills and have extra money. I bought a car and rented a house. I was drinking occasionally and went back to smoking pot full time.

In June of 2017, my adopted father died. I wasn't even mentioned and neither were my kids at his funeral even though I was the oldest kid. It was devastating because my adopted dad and I had made amends. We'd had a rocky relationship where we did not talk for several years, but we were good at the end. When I heard he was sick, I would call, but my stepmom would not return my calls. Everyone got to see him before he died except me. I was so hurt at the funeral. It was like I didn't count, again, and thrown away.

My adopted dad's friends, Jeff B. and Denny D., came up to me at the funeral and got my phone number. They called the next week and became my surrogate dads. They made sure I wasn't suicidal and met with me a week later. I asked for copies of any pictures there had of my adopted dad. They brought me a whole file folder full of their trips to Canada. My adopted dad was doing what he loved in those pictures, fishing. He had a huge smile on his face in each of the pictures.

Then Jeff B. called and said that Denny D. had Alzheimer's and was being placed in a care facility forty-five minutes away. We went to see him and still do. Even though Jeff and Denny were in my life, I began to drink whiskey daily to avoid the rage that I felt for my adopted dad's wife leaving me and my kids out of the funeral.

In April of 2018, my adopted mom died. I was crushed and continued drinking whiskey and smoking pot, though I quit smoking cigarettes in 2017.

Jesus

> *Jesus replied, "What is impossible for people is possible with God." (Luke 18:27 NLT)*

Early in 2019, I began searching for answers and Noah was put in my life. He was my friend's great-nephew and had also been adopted. We talked about adoption, how we felt, and openly discussed our feelings. During the course of one of our conversations, he told me about Jesus briefly and then asked if he could lay hands on me and pray. Thinking I had nothing to lose, I accepted. Little did I know that was the beginning of me having a relationship with Jesus.

Noah prayed over me. Instantly, I knew I needed to quit drinking and smoking pot. I suddenly had a conscience again. I couldn't get around the fact that Jesus was already working on my soul. During this time, all of the negative friends I had around me suddenly left me. It was all part of God's plan.

It took several weeks, but in April of 2019, I gave my life to Jesus. The change was instantaneous. I had no more cravings. My hard heart, the anger, and the rage left me. It was replaced with love. My focus was different now. I was calm, at peace, and filled with love.

The worst thing about closed adoptions is not knowing where you came from and not having people in your "family" that look, act, and sound like you. The mental effects are crippling even with good adoptive parents like mine. You are left trying to figure out "Why me?" God took that from me as well.

After I was saved, I heard a pastor on YouTube saying we are all adopted by our Heavenly Father. I thought, I can do this. I've been adopted once! I get this!

> *God decided in advance to adopt us into his own family by bringing us to himself through Jesus Christ. This is what he wanted to do, and it gave him great pleasure.*
> (Ephesians 1:4-5 NLT)

Now, I volunteer three days a week at a Prevention Center. I help with a curriculum that deals with substance abuse, bullying, and Social Emotional Learning. I help with anything they need me to do. The center was founded by a great friend of mine who I've known since 1981. He started the center in 1988.

I go to men's groups and a Bible study at the church. I host a Bible study at my apartment weekly as well. We start with food like Jesus did with the Apostles and then we get into the Word.

I am no longer dead inside. My depression, anxiety, and PTSD symptoms have all but left me. Only God's grace through Jesus could heal me. I used to sleep for an hour and a half and wake up with nightmares, then fall back asleep only to wake up again with night terrors in a pool of sweat. Now, I sleep much better! I can go into public now without looking over my shoulder. I am no longer bitter or judgmental. Through Jesus all things are possible.

Pause and Reflect...

Read Luke 1:37, Mark 10:27, and Matthew 19:26.

> *What amazing truth did Jesus reveal in all of these scriptures?*

Now read Matthew 17:20.

> *How does what Jesus told His disciples change how you can live your life and deal with life's trials?*
>
> *How does Ephesians 1:4-5 change your outlook on adoption?*

If you have not accepted Jesus as your Lord and Savior, we would recommend you do that today. It will change your life forever. All you need to do is confess that you have made mistakes in life, you are sorry for those mistakes, and ask Jesus to forgive you for them. Thank Him for dying on the cross for the forgiveness of your sins and ask Him to lead and guide you from this day forward.

CHAPTER 4
Dealing with Adoption Related Issues

Fears

So you have not received a spirit that makes you fearful slaves. Instead, you received God's Spirit when he adopted you as his own children. Now we call him, "Abba, Father." (Romans 8:15 NLT)

Noah

There were so many fears even after my adopted mom came into my life. I still had the fear of being alone and that I was not good enough for my family and my friends. I was afraid I would make the same mistakes as my dad when I was older. None of those fears were based on truth.

The truth is fear is buried beneath not trusting. I definitely had developed trust issues. However, fears are only fears until we overcome them by realizing we don't need to be afraid when we are loved. In fact, the Bible says perfect love casts out fear! (See 1 John 4:16-19.)

I would act happy around others so that people would think that I was fine. I even wanted to help others, not realizing I needed to help myself first. I just really wanted to act like something didn't happen, but it was incredibly hard to do that because I felt so alone. It was like I knew there were people that loved me and cared about me, but there was this huge hole in my heart that needed deep surgery so I could trust them. I longed to meet my birth mom, but it was in the wrong, unhealthy way. I had convinced myself that if I met her, all my fears would go away. Once I discovered this was not the answer, I knew I was hurting deep in my heart.

The only answer for overcoming my fear was to trust God. When He said He loved me and that nothing I can do could make Him leave me, I had to hold onto that truth and not let my heart become filled with doubt. God's heart surgery comes in unexpected ways and continues in my life even to this day.

He is the great physician and knows exactly what we need to heal that hole in our hearts!

Pause and Reflect...

One of the ways God used to help me was through His Word. There are so many scriptures about trusting Him. I began to read them and commit them to memory. If doubt tried to worm its way back into my thinking, I could shut it down by quoting one of the verses I had memorized.

First read Romans 8:31, 33, 35, and 37-39.

Meditate on these amazing truths that will help you shut out doubt and begin to trust your loving Heavenly Father.

Start with the two scriptures below. Write out memorize each one. Repeat one of them out loud to yourself all throughout your day for one week. As you fill your mind and heart with the truth of His Word, you will see your fear of trusting begin to fade away.

Psalm 56:3-4

_____

_____

Proverbs 3:5-6

_____

_____

Once you have memorized these two scriptures, look for others that fill your heart with God's love for you.

> *We know how much God loves us, and we have put our trust in his love. God is love, and all who live in love live in God, and God lives in them. And as we live in God, our love grows more perfect. So we will not be afraid on the day of judgment, but we can face him with confidence because we live like Jesus here in this world. Such love has no fear, because perfect love expels all fear. If we are afraid, it is for fear of punishment, and this shows that we have not fully experienced his perfect love. We love each other because he loved us first. (1 John 4:16-19 NLT)*

Scot

> *For God has not given us a spirit of fear, but of power and of love and of a sound mind. (2 Timothy 1:7 NKJV)*

My fears were always, "You're not good enough. If people knew you, they wouldn't like you. They're only nice to you because they feel sorry for you." As I got older it was, "You don't deserve to be loved." Fear brought out hate in me. I hated other races, people who were different from me, and even my high school classmates. Fear is False Evidence Appearing Real. Jesus took that from me when I got saved and filled me with His love, His power, and gave me a sound mind. I'm not perfect, but I have discernment from the Holy Spirit so fear no longer cripples me.

Pause and Reflect...

Isaiah 41:10 says, "Don't be afraid, for I am with you. Don't be discouraged, for I am your God. I will strengthen you and help you. I will hold you up with my victorious right hand" (NLT).

> *How does this promise from God assist you in dealing with your personal fears?*

I suggest you copy this verse and post it where you can read it every morning as you start your day and then read it again before you go to bed at night.

Also remember: Fear is False Evidence Appearing Real.

Forgiveness

> *"If you forgive those who sin against you, your heavenly Father will forgive you. But if you refuse to forgive others, your Father will not forgive your sins."*
> (Jesus in Matthew 6:14-15 NLT)

Noah

The struggle of forgiveness is long and difficult and incredibly painful at times. Jesus calls us to forgive 7x70 times (see Luke 17:4). That's just a metaphor meaning we need to forgive a lot. Forgiveness is a journey. However, after you truly forgive someone, there is this freedom from the unbearable weight of unforgiveness you have carried. It causes hurt and puts your heart in a tangle.

However, being free and becoming free are two different things. **Becoming free** can take a lifetime if you try to earn that freedom in your own strength. Why try to earn something that is already yours? **Being free** is letting God handle the things you can't control.

God says you're already free because Jesus is your Lord and Savior. You see, Jesus not only saved you and forgave you from your sins, He also gave you the power and love to forgive others. Filling your heart with His love helps you to see others as He sees them. Just like you did not have to earn His forgiveness and love, neither do those who have hurt you.

What does "being free" mean? At first, I struggled with that. If God says that is true but I don't believe it, that would mean God would have unfinished business. Of course, He does not have unfinished business. He finished what needed to be done on the cross. In fact, Jesus said so just before He died on the cross, "It is finished!" He fulfilled the requirement and He paid the full price once and for all for our freedom.

1 Timothy 2:6 says, "He gave his life to purchase freedom for everyone. This is the message God gave to the world at just the right time" (NLT).

Jesus said He came to set us free, so we are truly free. When you hurt and feel there is nowhere to go, remember Jesus came to set you free.

It was for this freedom that Christ set us free [completely liberating us]; therefore keep standing firm and do not be subject again to a yoke of slavery [which you once removed]. (Galatians 5:1 AMP)

Also know from God's Word that when we forgive others, there is freedom (see Galatians 5:13). When we find freedom, we find a whole new world. Imagine you did something terrible like kill someone. You go to prison for that. You are in there for fifty years. When you get out after fifty years, you spend your whole life regretting your past. However, once you got out of that prison, you realize you can smell the flowers, feel the wind, and see people. You do not want to ever go back to prison ever again.

This is what happens when Christ gives us a life of freedom. When we forgive, we are set free. We can smell the flowers again. We are not trapped in a self-imposed prison of unforgiveness and bitterness. We are free because we forgave as Christ forgave us.

When God gives us this freedom, it's a sustainable promise that He will fulfill.

Galatians 3:22 says, "But the Scriptures declare that we are all prisoners of sin, so we receive God's promise of freedom only by believing in Jesus Christ" (NLT).

Scot

First, I had to be willing to forgive myself before I could forgive anyone else. However, I couldn't do that before I surrendered to Jesus. I would continually beat myself up over the things I had done or said to myself or to other people. Jesus took the burden off me when He forgave me of my sins. Now, I need to forgive people where they are at and not be judgmental towards them. An attitude of forgiveness is continually at the forefront of my thoughts, especially since I was so unforgiving for so many years.

Pause and Reflect...

Read Galatians 5:13.

> *What does this verse say you are called to do?*
>
> *What are you to use the freedom Christ has given you to do?*

Read Romans 6:14.

> *What is no longer your master?*
>
> *What do you live under now?*
>
> *How have our stories impacted your handling of fear and forgiveness?*

Thoughts About My Birth Mom

> *Even if my father and mother abandon me, the LORD will hold me close.* (Psalm 27:10 NLT)

Noah

There are two things that could happen when and if I get to meet my birth mom. I know this because God has shown me them in a crazy way. I had two dreams about what could happen.

In one of the dreams, I was in a coffee shop. I don't know where the coffee shop was or why I was there in this dream. I was sitting there and this woman approached me. I was very confused because I didn't know why she was approaching me.

She then gave me a hug and said, "I am Andrea, your birth mom."

I began to weep. We then talked. She was interested in my life, my family, my dreams, and my hopes. We cried and laughed a lot. The moment seemed to go on for hours.

She then asked, "Noah, why aren't you mad at me?"

I said, "I don't need to be mad or angry at you because you're loved by the One that sets you free."

She said she was sorry for everything that she had done, and then she said, "Noah, I want to accept Jesus in my heart and become a difference-maker in the world."

It was like my entire soul was just bursting out into tears at that moment. It was life-long dream come true. After a sleepless night of praying for her, it all became so worth it to me. It was so amazing and so much like the movies.

I get emotional thinking about both dreams. For different reasons, though—one good and one bad.

The second dream is harder to write. Every time I write it, I have a lot of emotions that are hard to process. I was at the same coffee shop as the one in the first dream. This woman approached me. I didn't know who or why this woman was there, but she sat down with me.

Then she says, "Noah, you were never worth it to me. You were a piece of crap."

She just sits there and continues to belittle me and wrecks me. Not only that, she was the same as people had told me she was when I was born. She started telling me about my brother and how she gave him up because he wasn't worth it, either. I just started to weep because I didn't know what to say to all of that. I ran out of that coffee shop and just cried out to God.

These were just dreams. I know there is always hope for my birth mom to change, but it's her decision, her life. I am not out to change her, I just want to plant a seed of what Jesus could do in her life. I say this with tears in my eyes because my hope is that she will see that seed is worth it.

My biggest desire is for someone to plant a seed in the hurting the people like her that are on drugs, have abusive parents, are prostitutes, are gang members, and criminals.

Of course, my hope is that the first dream is what happens if I do get to meet with my birth mom, but I know if the second one happens, that's not who I am. I am not her mistakes. Her mistakes don't define me as a person and they never did. God defines who I am. He is the one who created me and knew me even when I was in her womb.

Scot

When I was younger, I had a deep desire to meet my biological mom. I would wonder what she would say about giving me up for adoption and how she would answer my questions. Why couldn't I stay with you? Why did you give me up? Wasn't I good enough?

Then I realized all of those were selfish questions. When I had kids of my own, I tried to find out about her because I wanted a medical history to pass on to them. I do still wonder what she's like, but it is no longer an obsession. I can't imagine giving up my kids for adoption. What I come up with is it must have been the hardest and most emotional thing for her to do. I am grateful for the life she gave me by denying herself the experience of having me in her life.

Pause and Reflect...

We both had to learn that it is God who defines who we are. He is the one who created us and knew us even when we were still in our mother's womb. Not only did He know us, He had a plan and purpose for us.

Read Psalm 139:13-16.

What assurances do you get from these verses?

What impact do these verses have on how you see yourself?

Carefully begin to monitor your self-talk. Make sure what you are saying about yourself lines us with what God says about you. Read the following verses and describe what God is saying about you.

Ephesian 1:6 says I am

_____

_____

John 15:16 says I have been

_____

_____

Genesis 1:26 says I was created

_____

_____

Ephesians 2:10 says I am His

_____

_____

2 Peter 1:4 says I am a partaker of

_____

_____

1 Peter 2:4 says I am

_____

_____

Romans 8:16 says I am

_____

_____

CHAPTER 5
Community Comparison Identity

Noah

Community is so important to healing. Not only to heal yourself, but also to help others heal. We all are all broken, so we all need others and God daily. We need to have people that can pick us up when we are down. Ever since the beginning of time, God did not just make one but two people because man is never good alone. The same is true today. We need to have good people to walk with and talk to and that will challenge our hearts and thoughts.

I struggle with vulnerability. Even writing this book is painful for me. It is definitely challenging me. However, it's also helping me heal and grow.

We all need interaction with others, but with not just any community. We need a true, authentic community where we can be real. That's where it starts. We may find it hard at first to find an authentic community, but it is worth the effort to choose wisely.

We can't love Jesus without others supporting us, loving us, and sharing with us. We can't love Jesus on our own. Remember, Jesus said we are to love our neighbor as ourselves (see Matthew 19:19). That is how we show others the love we have for Jesus and the love He has for them (see John 13:35). Community is what makes us grow into the person God has called us to be.

There are people in our authentic community that desperately love us and need us to love them. Every single decision I have ever made, for better or for worse, people of my community were there praying for me. There are people praying over you that you may not even know about. God made us to be with one another and to build one another up.

Being in a community makes us part of the body of Christ. We may be a finger, a hand, or a part of the heart. A body has many different parts (see 1 Corinthians 12:14-27). In a community, it's the same concept. The different parts make up one body/community. A community does not have to be in a church. A community can start anywhere. When I first stepped into being part of a community, it was in a high school classroom.

However, as you choose your community, do it so it is worth the time, energy, and money to be an active participant. Where authenticity happens is where true healing happens. I firmly believe in community. Ever since the beginning of time, God designed us to have someone with us. God created Adam, but then God said it was not good for man to be alone. So, what did God do? He created a woman so that man would not be alone (see Genesis 2:18-22).

Jesus walked with twelve people. Three of those people walked more closely with Jesus than the others. He calls us to do the same. Yes, it is important to have personal quiet times, but if you look at Jesus' life and ministry, He was with people the majority of the time. He walked with people that believed in Him, but would also challenge Him.

To really change your heart, find people that will love you and guide you throughout your life. We are never meant to be alone.

Pause and Reflect...

Review the scriptures suggested in this section for further information on the importance of being part of an authentic community. Record what you learn from each passage.

Genesis 2:18-22

Matthew 19:19

John 13:35

1 Corinthians 12:14-27

Genesis 2:18-22

_____

_____

Scot

When I was in grade school, middle school, and high school, my community was my peers. However, I found myself always comparing my insides to their outsides and always came up as less than them.

After High School, I was in the Air Force and they became my community. After basic training, I felt the best I had ever felt. I made it through boot camp where others in the community challenged me to continually improve physically. I got to where I could run two miles without stopping. Those nagging derogatory thoughts briefly left me.

However, when I got to my permanent duty station, I quickly reverted and again compared my insides with other's outsides. Negative thoughts flooded me unless I was drunk or high which seemed to be any time I was off duty.

After my discharge, I had no community until I went into AA. They are a good organization, however, I always felt less than the others again and not quite good enough. It seemed it was based on how much sobriety you had and who your sponsor was.

When I got into the VA system, I had hope I could be whole again. The problem was I was still fearful and full of rage. I felt comfortable in the Domiciliary during my three-month stints. It wasn't the real world, but I would feel good and not have as many outbursts.

It wasn't until I became part of a church community and gave my life to Jesus that I was able to be part of a "real" community.

This community brought inner healing and continually challenged me to grow and mature in a healthy productive way. My identity now is one of God's beloved children! I am a member of His kingdom community.

Pause and Reflect...

Read 1 John 5:1.

> *What does this verse say you are?*

Read Romans 8:16-17.

> *How do these verses identify you?*

Philippians 3:20.

> *Where does this say your citizenship is located?*

Compassion

> *The LORD is compassionate and merciful, slow to get angry and filled with unfailing love.* (Psalm 103:8 NLT)

Noah

I also struggle with this thing called compassion. I discovered this was because I was comparing myself to another person. This didn't get me anywhere when it came to establishing loving relationships. Comparing myself to others only made me feel worse about myself which, of course, put me on the defensive. It is hard to feel compassion for another when we are trying to become something we were never designed to become.

We are all designed to be part of a community, but we are also like snowflakes. We are all different. Every snowflake is unique. We each have our own story that will impact someone else. So, we aren't to compare our story to anyone else's. God is still writing mine. He is still writing yours as well.

To compare yourself to someone else, you're literally taking the experience God has designed for you and redesigning it using someone else's pen. Comparing yourself to others kills your joy. Be your own snowflake and let others do the same.

But they, measuring themselves by themselves, and comparing themselves among themselves, are not wise. (2 Corinthians 10:12 NKJV)

I used to think Andrea's mistakes defined me. I thought because she had me, I would mess up like her. I used to think that the way she destroyed her life defined my life as well. None of that is true. Sadly, that way of thinking caused a lot of self-blame and low self-esteem in my heart. I used to think because I was adopted, I was a mistake. That was false as well. I didn't realize that I was not a mistake until Jesus came into my life.

It breaks my heart to write this, but I am trying to be transparent about my life so it will help others walking a similar path. Before I understood God's love and had a relationship with Him through Jesus Christ, I felt like I was two different people. I was one person who would go to church and Bible studies, but I felt like I could not be authentic with other Christians because of where I was at the time. My identity was in worldly satisfaction or what I thought could fill me up. I would act like a good Christian, but then go to parties. The wild thing about it all was I could not get drunk or mess around with women. The fact that God saved me from that was insane, but I see now He was watching over me even when I was not aware of it.

I strongly regret the decisions I made during that time in my life, but I would not trade them for anything. What those experiences taught me was my identity is not in the world's definition of satisfaction but in being enough for Christ. I wish I could have learned that sooner, but now I know I'd rather be my own person.

I am no longer a slave to what my birth mom thinks about me. I am no longer bound to selfishness. I don't want to live my life faking it, but as authentically as I can. My identity is no longer in what people think, but in what Jesus has already done for me.

Jesus adopts us all into His arms and then begins making us more like Him every day. He allows us to come back to Him every evening and shows us how to clean up after being in the world. Does that allow us to keep sinning? No! It puts a higher standard for us to reach for so we do not sin. We need that fresh reminder every day and sometimes more than once a day.

Another aspect of adoption is it takes place when someone **chooses** to love you. Love is always a choice. We are not only getting adopted, but when we are sharing God's love, we are "adopting" others into the kingdom of God.

Getting adopted is about love, but there is still pain. The moment we get adopted, we become part of God's family, but life gets harder not easier. It's harder because we are entering the process of becoming a new person. We are a masterpiece being created in the image of our Heavenly Father. It takes time to become a completed masterpiece. To be a completed masterpiece in Jesus will not fully happen until we go to heaven. While we are on the earth, Jesus is still creating and molding us into His likeness.

For we are God's masterpiece. He has created us anew in Christ Jesus, so we can do the good things he planned for us long ago. (Ephesians 2:10 NLT)

Just as it takes months and even years for a master to build a magnificent and beautiful masterpiece, it's the same thing with the kingdom of God. The Bible tells us God knew all about us while we were still in our birth mother's womb. Even then He had a plan and purpose designed for our life. We have always been a masterpiece in God's mind, but to become it takes time. It takes "redos" as we grow and mature into His perfect design. We will never be a completed masterpiece until we join Him in heaven, but for now, we are a masterpiece in God's eyes being continually perfected through our experiences here on the earth.

Scot

Compassion for me is simple. It's the opposite of being judgmental of others. I have judged people all my life and it got me a sick, hard heart. I still struggle with compassion in my daily life because I have judged people for so long. It is the first thing that pops into my head. I have to reprimand myself and say, "No! That person has the same feelings and desires I do. Don't judge them. I am to love them!"

Compassion to me is also being in tune with God and how He loved everyone. I am working on loving everyone through daily practice. I ask the Lord to show me others the way He sees them so that I can reflect His compassion towards them.

Pause and Reflect...

What does Psalm 103:13 tell you about God's relationship to you as His child?

How does Joel 2:13 describe God?

How has learning this about your Heavenly Father changed your attitude toward others?

Noah

We are to show compassion to one another and not be judgmental, however, there is such a thing as righteous anger. That is different than being judgmental. Being judgmental is a sin. Righteous anger is anger that is not sinful. It usually has to do with taking action against injustice. I am so full of righteous anger when it comes to how abuse, drugs, and abandonment hurt kids. I am thankful for the foster care system that helps children whose lives are forever changed by other people's decisions. Sadly, social injustices are always going to happen because of sin, but God still leads us to help the broken and brokenhearted.

I want to reach the people that have similar or worse circumstances than I have experienced. It's not to show them that I am better, but because I am the same as they are because of what I have experienced in my life. We can learn from every single person's story.

I have righteous anger and desperately want to be the "church" for the broken. It's not the healthy but the sick and broken that need to know the love of Jesus. I feel called to be "the church." I mean we are "the church." We're the mission on a mission or looking for a mission.

I am just an ordinary person, but my God is extraordinary. I desperately want to be used so much for this and to make an impact on these broken and abandoned people.

It is so important that we teach them to continue to walk forward because if we don't, we will be stuck in our past. I want to walk people out of the dark places and walk with them into the light.

My heart breaks for the injustices I see all around us. This is not a political stance. This is my heart breaking. My heart hurts for the people that hurt because hurting people hurt other people. These are the people that kill and rape. My heart breaks for them because uncontrolled hurt develops anger which can manifest in rage and self-destructive behavior.

Not only does my heart break for them, but when they say that I am too young to make a difference in the world, that is a huge lie. I have a voice. I know I am not enough without Jesus and that I can't change people. I can only plant a seed that will start a legacy.

However, when people come to me with hurt and deep wounds, I need to remind myself I am not their savior. I need to allow the Holy Spirit to break in and guide me to truly help them find the answers they need. The Holy Spirit is so important when we are making ourselves available to help others. We have the same power as Jesus, but only Jesus can save and heal people. We are just the messengers of His work. In fact, the Bible says we are Christ's ambassadors, His personal representatives (see 2 Corinthians 5:20). God is using us to make His appeal to them. However, we must remember our authority comes only from Him.

So many times, we want to put the blame of the injustices of others on leadership. Why is the leader not doing this or that? God created us all for His mission field. It's not about the next political party or the guy that won't stand up. God says He created us to go into the world to make a difference. We are His church. The church is good for the community we are part of and to help us and others grow. However, the church is the people not the building. We are not called to remain in the four walls of a church building. In fact, the early churches were in tents so they could be mobile and go where they were needed to help others.

Jesus came to not only fix the brokenness in people, but to fix the broken systems that were ultimately created for good, but have been destroyed because of sin. Sin separates us, destroys us, and puts up a barrier around us to keep us trapped and unable to fulfill our mission. Jesus says goodbye to barriers and hello to new life (see Ephesians 2:14-16).

He has equipped us to fulfill our mission. What is better, to give a man a fish or teach the man how to fish. If you teach a man to fish, then he can then teach others to fish. Jesus told His disciples He was going to make them fisher of men (see Mark 1:17). That means, when things happen in your life that are unfair, Jesus uses them to draw others to Him through your testimony. What could be more unfair than God's own Son being crucified on a cross because of trumped-up charges and lies? Jesus said if He was lifted up (on the cross) He would draw all men to Him (see John 12:32).

I don't want to just sit around all my life waiting for God to do something He has called and equipped me to do. If I spend my whole life waiting, then I have just wasted my life. I want to be used by God. It does not start when I am older or when I have a college degree. The displaced were as young as sixteen. I want to be used every single day for His kingdom purposes. God's greatest mission is love and that should be ours as well. The Great Commission Jesus gave all of us as His disciples was to take His good news into all the world (see Mark 16:15).

Pause and Reflect...

> *What is that Good News spoken of in Mark 16:15 that we are to take into all the world?*

Read Mark 16:16-20.

> *What is the rest of our mission?*

> *What did Jesus mean in Mark 1:17 when He said He would make us fishers of men?*

> *Explain what it means to be Christ's ambassador (2 Corinthians 5:20).*

Scot

My righteous anger comes from the abortion issue. I think it should be outlawed. It also rises up within me when I see kids that are abandoned, abused, or are in foster care that have no voice. I pray for them all.

Pause and Reflect...

Define righteous anger

_____

_____

What do you feel righteous anger about?

_____

_____

What can you do about righting what you believe is wrong?

_____

_____

CHAPTER 6
Satan Exists

Noah

My all-time favorite Bible verse is John 10:10. "The thief does not come except to steal, and to kill, and to destroy. I have come that they may have life, and that they may have *it* more abundantly" (NKJV).

The kingdom of darkness has been trying to invade my life so I know that Satan is real. He set out to kill, steal, and destroy my life.

He started with fear. He wants to put fear in you that you're all alone and fills you with the fear of no one loving you. The list of fears that the enemy puts on you is endless. He wants to make you fearful so you cannot function effectively in life.

I am not just talking about mental illness. I am talking about the fear of anything that the enemy puts on you. Every fear the enemy puts on you is just another way for you to learn to trust God. Jesus conquered fear and every other form of spiritual oppression on the cross for you.

We should be the most fearless people on earth, but in our western culture, we don't really understand spiritual practices. We don't see that spiritual oppression is a real thing just like the presence of Jesus. There are demons. They are real spiritual spirits that bring fear. The Bible tells us our fight is not against other people but against the rulers, authorities, powers, and forces of evil.

Satan also uses pride to try and move us away from a true relationship with God. Satan literally used to sit next to God. He was called Lucifer which means son of the morning, but his pride made him want to become God (see Isaiah 14:12-13). We cannot become God. Pride is so cancerous and can keep us from loving and helping others.

In fact, the Bible warns us, "God opposes the proud but favors the humble. So humble yourselves before God." Then it goes on to assure us, "Resist the devil, and he will flee from you. Come close to God, and he will come close to you" (James 4:6-8 NLT).

God wants us to be aware of our enemy the devil, but He also wants us to know that Jesus defeated him on the cross, so we do not have to let the enemy have the victory over us.

1 John 3:8 says, "The Son of God came to destroy the works of the devil" (NLT).

However, we still have to be aware of the enemy and understand he will try to deceive us. 1 Peter 5:8 also warns us, "Stay alert! Watch out for your great enemy, the devil. He prowls around like a roaring lion, looking for someone to devour" (NLT).

Jesus was Himself tempted by the devil, but He showed us how to deal with the enemy's tactics. "Get out of here, **Satan**," Jesus told him. "For the Scriptures say, 'You must worship the Lord your God and serve only him'" (Matthew 4:10 NLT).

Pause and Reflect...

There are a number of scriptures that tell us how we can avoid being deceived and tricked by our adversary, the devil.

Read Ephesians 6:10-18 that explains the Armor of God and how to use it in our spiritual battles against Satan.

List each piece of the armor, what it is for, and how to use.

_____

_____

_____

_____

_____

_____

Read the advice the Apostle Paul gave in 2 Timothy 2:22-26.

What did you learn that will help you personally from these verses?

How can you use what you have learned to help others who may not understand the spiritual battles we may have to face in life?

Scot

Fear used to run my entire life. I was always afraid that someone or something was going to get me. I was afraid my friends would leave me. I was afraid to try new things. I was frozen in fear. During my elementary school years, I would show it outwardly. It came out as nervous energy. In middle school, I hid it. I wanted friends, but I didn't know how to be one or get one. I would tell myself, "They are just being nice to you. You are not worth it." This just caused more "false evidence appearing real." In high school, my fear became outward rage.

Now I know Jesus has got my back and these are all unfounded fears that my loving Heavenly Father does not want me to experience. In fact, He has given me two of the most amazing promises on which to base my life.

"And be sure of this: I am with you always, even to the end of the age" (Jesus in Matthew 28:20 NLT).

"So be strong and courageous! Do not be afraid and do not panic before them. For the LORD your God will personally go ahead of you. He will neither fail you nor abandon you" (Deuteronomy 31:6 NLT).

Pause and Reflect...

> *Can you relate to any of the fears I faced in my life growing up?*
>
> *How did they affect the choices you made as a young adult?*
>
> *How does knowing God will never forsake you and that Jesus has got your back help you deal with these fears?*

Shame

> *Instead of shame and dishonor, you will enjoy a double share of honor. You will possess a double portion of prosperity in your land, and everlasting joy will be yours. (Isaiah 61:7 NLT)*

Noah

Another way that the enemy comes against us is through deeply rooted shame. Shame is disgracing and dishonoring yourself and taking all the blame on your shoulders.

We do cause shame in our lives even without Satan attacking because we sin, but Satan will use that shame to come between us and others and between us and Jesus. However, when Satan comes at us, we must remember he was defeated by Jesus when He died on the cross. In fact, Jesus said He came to destroy the works of Satan. When we do not understand Satan exists, we allow him to get a foothold, attack, and overtake us. We know that God protects us, but we need to learn how to use the weapons God has given us against this enemy (review Ephesians 6:10-18).

We also do this by taking every thought captive that tries to come in and fill us with shame. The best way to do this is to declare the truths of what God says about us.

Do not receive the negative, shameful thoughts the enemy tries to fill your mind with. Instead, boldly tell him what God has said about you.

Scot

Guilt is about behavior, a feeling of conscience from having done something wrong that is against your values. Shame is a feeling of badness about yourself. Toxic shame is a feeling of worthlessness, humiliation, and self-loathing. It is a paralyzing feeling that afflicts one through repeated traumatic experiences, often but not always, rooted in childhood trauma and experiences.

I first felt guilty that I couldn't please my parents. Then it became shame, then toxic shame. I spent years in therapy getting rid of toxic shame. First, I would do something wrong, feel guilty, then it would turn to shame and I would tell myself, "See you're no good." Then the cycle would start all over. This went on clear into my adulthood until I asked Jesus to come into my life. I was dead inside because of toxic shame. Now, I no longer beat myself up over mistakes. I acknowledge my mistake, ask for forgiveness, and go on. I don't dwell on my mistakes knowing once I ask Him,

Jesus will forgive me and I can move forward and complete the mission He has for my life.

Pause and Reflect...

Guilt and shame can paralyze us and keep us bound so we cannot move forward with our God-given assignments.

The enemy loves to remind us of our mistakes. However, once we understand God's forgiveness, we can learn from our mistakes and become even more productive in serving Him.

List the mistakes Satan keeps reminding you of.

After you ask Jesus to forgive you for that mistake, cross it off with a red pen, and thank Him for forgiving you. If the enemy tries to bring it up again, show him the list with each one crossed off.

Remember, only what God says about you is the truth. Satan only knows how to lie because he is the father of lies.

Pride

For the world offers only a craving for physical pleasure, a craving for everything we see, and pride in our achievements and possessions. These are not from the Father, but are from this world. (1 John 2:16 NLT)

Scot

Pride hardened my heart so much that even though I had low self-esteem, I was very prideful. "I'm not wrong you are! It's not my fault. I'm better than you because no one is as smart as I am." I was the best counselor. I was the best business analyst. Pride also kept me from me needing Jesus. When I realized how prideful I was and how that kept me from realizing my potential from God, I repented. I still struggle with pride, but I know immediately when it happens. I take care of it right away.

Pause and Reflect...

I learned some important lessons about what pride does. Here are some of the scriptures that helped me.

Proverbs 11:2 says, "Pride leads to _____, but with humility comes _____.

Proverbs 13:10 says, "Pride leads to _____; those who take _____ are wise.

Proverbs 16:18 warns, "Pride goes before _____, and haughtiness before a _____."

Proverbs 29:23 tells us, "Pride ends in _____, while _____ brings honor.

Separation from God

For since our friendship with God was restored by the death of his Son while we were still his enemies, we will certainly be saved through the life of his Son. So now we can rejoice in our wonderful new relationship with God because our Lord Jesus Christ has made us friends of God. (Romans 5:10-11 NLT)

Another reason Satan attacks us is because he wants us to be completely separated from God in every way possible. Satan is the ruler of darkness, a fallen angel from Heaven. Satan comes to attack us, but Jesus is becoming my best friend. What He has done for me, He will do for you as well. All you need to do is turn to Him.

Pause and Reflect...

We were both like the Prodigal Son Jesus talked about in the parable in Luke 15:11-32. We suggest you read through this and see how you relate to what the rebellious son chose to do and how the loving father treated him when he returned home after losing everything.

What did this son ask his father to give him?

Why did he want it?

What did he do when his father gave it to him?

What did he find out about the world when all of his money ran out?

What did he say to himself when he "came to his senses"?

What was the father doing all the time his son was gone?

How do we know that?

What did he do when he saw his son coming up the road?

Even though the boy was dirty, had ragged clothing, and smelled like a pigpen, what did his father do?

Who did Jesus say the father in the story represented?

CONCLUSION
God's Faithfulness

For the law was given through Moses, but God's unfailing love and faithfulness came through Jesus Christ. (John 1:17 NLT)

Noah

God has been so faithful in my life that I can tell you a lot about His faithfulness. I see God's hand on my life through my family and the way He now uses this story to help others.

God's protection has always been something super present in my life. When I was younger and I did not know who or what my birth mom was or what she did, my earthly father protected me and provided for me. He protected me from getting abused. He protected me from the lies that my birth mom was telling. He worked two jobs to make ends meet. My dad and my whole family love Jesus.

I don't know how to describe how God used my earthly father without tears coming in my eyes. While he was providing for us and could not protect us, there was always someone there. When it wasn't my dad, it was my nana and papa. At one point, my nana and papa were even going to adopt me to remove me from that volatile situation. God had a plan of protecting me even when I did not understand. My dad would do anything for his kids then and even today.

I know deep down inside, my earthly father and my adoptive mother would do anything for me just like Christ would do for me. That kind of parenting is not easy because caring for me was not easy. I made mistakes every single day. I failed and came across challenges that I could comprehend. I was diagnosed with depression, anxiety, and a learning disability. In third grade, I was having thoughts of suicide. They stopped because my parents got me the help I needed and I started taking medication for it. I hated taking pills and over the years, I have weaned off them little by little. I still take medication today, but I know God is going to continue to wean me off them. I fully understand that it is a medical problem.

I also know that having a medical problem will not stop God from moving and being faithful in my life. God never created depression, anxiety, or worry. None of that is from God. Yet, we tend to blame God because we want to blame someone, but He did not create us to be like that. When we look at the kingdom of God and see it's the opposite of the world. I thank God for Jesus who redeems all things! Jesus has been all over the place in my life. He has even helped me write my part of this book as a way to help others.

Pause and Reflect...

> *What are the wonderful promises of God's love and faithfulness in Psalm 89:2 and Psalm 117:2?*

Look back over your own life and see how God has revealed His faithfulness.

Scot

Great is his faithfulness; his mercies begin afresh each morning. (Lamentations 3:23 NLT)

It is obvious to me now how faithful God has been to me. What I know for sure is I should've been dead many times from drug overdoses, alcohol poisonings, suicide attempts, and car wrecks. I know my adopted mom prayed for me every day. She had a relationship with God that was unbreakable.

God had a plan for me, but I was unwilling to follow Him until April of 2019. My adopted mom never saw me saved. I thought a lot about her and my grandma who was my adopted father's mother. She too was very religious and spiritual. They were best friends.

Through Jesus, I'm learning what it is to be faithful, truthful in all I do, and keeping my word. He has taught me that yes means yes and no means no.

I have a hard time comprehending the faithfulness of God, but I'm glad He waited for me. Now, I can start each day in His presence and know He is there for me as I go throughout my day.

Jesus has been my faithful friend who sticks closer to me than a brother (Proverbs 18:24).

Pause and Reflect...

Read Psalm 25:10.

> *What promise does God give you in this verse?*

Read Psalm 33:4.

> *What does this say about God's Word and His work?*

Read Psalm 91:4.

> *What did you learn about God's faithfulness from this verse?*

Read Psalm 100:5.

> *What amazing promise does God give you in this verse?*

Pray this prayer: *Guide me in Your truth and faithfulness and teach me, for You are the God of my salvation; for You only do I expectantly wait all day long. I thank You for your mercy, loving-kindness, and faithfulness.*

APPENDIX 1
Children Ask Questions

Children ask questions to figure out the world. If a child's family was formed by adoption, much of his or her curiosity will center on birth mothers, babies, and the reasons adoption plans are made. We've compiled 20 of the most frequently asked questions, from the preschooler's, "Did I grow in your tummy?" to the more complex queries preteens and teens may voice, along with sound responses suggested by experts and other parents over the years. As you talk to your child, adapt the sample language to fit your family's circumstances.

1. "Did I grow in your tummy?"

"No, you didn't grow in my tummy. You grew in your birth mother's tummy, and then you were born. When your birth mother and birth father were expecting you, they knew that they couldn't take care of any baby at that time. Your birth mother found us, and we became your parents. I'm so happy that we are! That is called adoption."

Although very young children can't yet understand reproduction, it's important to introduce the birth father from your earliest conversations. Your child also needs to understand that she was born, just like any other baby. Some parents skip that step, saying,

"No, you didn't grow in my tummy. We adopted you!" This leads the child to believe "I wasn't born, I was adopted."

2. "Why didn't my birth parents keep me?"

"Sometimes when a man and a woman have a baby, they cannot take care of any child at that time. It's never because of anything wrong about the child. It's for grownup reasons. Babies need a lot of care, day and night. They need healthy food, a warm place to sleep, to be cared for when they're sick, and to have grownups hold them when they cry. Your birth parents knew they couldn't provide all of these things, so they looked for a family that could."

3. "Was my birth mommy sad?"

"Your birth mother was sad to say goodbye, but she knew she couldn't take care of you and provide all the things babies need. She was happy that she was doing her best for you by finding our family to adopt you. She had both sad and happy tears."

Hearing directly from their birth parents can help children. If you don't remain in contact but were with your child's birth mother at the hospital or court, tell your child what she said. If you have a letter your child's birth mother wrote, share it with him.

4. "I wish I had grown in your tummy."

"You sound sad about that. That's OK. Sometimes I wish you had grown in my tummy, too, but I feel as close to you as if you had. I love you so much."

Don't be alarmed if your child displays sadness when she first begins to process adoption. In the preschool years, children want nothing more than to be as close as possible to their mothers. Some sadness, or even anger, is a normal reaction, and a way for a very young child to express her love for you, the mother she knows and loves.

5. "Why did you adopt me?"

"Daddy and I couldn't make a baby, but we wanted a baby to love very much. You were born from your birth mother's tummy, but she couldn't take care of any baby at that time. You were ready for a mommy and daddy, and we were ready for you. So, we adopted you and became a forever family."

6. "How do birth mommies make babies?"

"It takes a man and a woman to make a baby. Your birth father's sperm and your birth mother's egg combined inside her uterus to form an embryo. The embryo grows inside the woman, who then gives birth to the baby. You were born the same way any other baby is born. Some babies always live with the people who give birth to them, like your friend, _____, but others go to new parents, like you. That's called adoption."

7. "What happened the day I was born?"

"When your birth mother knew it was almost time for you to be born, she called us and we rushed to the hospital. We got there in time to be in the delivery room! We watched you being born and we held you as soon as the doctor delivered you. Your birth mother held you and said you were beautiful. You were always with us, your birth mother, or a nurse when you were in the hospital; you were never alone there."

If you have a photo from that day, show it to your child. Say something like "Here you are with Ellen on the day you were born."

If you don't have any information about your child's birth, you can explain what conditions were probably like where he was born.

8. "Was I a bad baby? Did I cry too much?"

"No. All babies are supposed to cry. That's how they tell us that they're hungry or tired or need to be changed. And adoption is never the child's fault. Adoption plans are made for grownup reasons, usually because the baby's birth parents can't take care of the baby and provide what he or she needs."

9. "What does my birth mother look like?"

If you have a picture, show it to your child. If you don't, but have met her, describe what she looked like. If you don't know, you can say, "She probably looks a lot like you, so she must be very beautiful." Together, imagine what she might look like, or invite your child to draw a picture.

10. "I wish I could ask my birth mother _____."

"I'm going to write a letter to your birth mother next week. Do you want me to include that question, or do you want to write your own letter to send with mine?" [Or, if you're not in touch with your child's birth mother] "Why don't you write to your birth mother and ask her that question, and any others on your mind? We can send the letter to your adoption agency. They may not know where she is, so she may not get the letter, but if they do know where she is, I'm sure she'd be glad to hear from you."

11. "Maybe my birth mother was a princess."

"That's exciting to imagine, isn't it? But there aren't many princesses in North Dakota, so I think she's probably like most people, working hard at a job."

Many children, not just those who were adopted, fantasize about an alternate set of "perfect" parents. Encourage your child to talk about these fantasies, but present the concrete information you have about her birth parents.

12. "Why is my skin brown and your skin pink?"

"You were born to birth parents [or to a woman] who have the same beautiful brown skin color as yours. I was born to Grandma and Grandpa, who have the same skin color as mine. We usually inherit our skin color, hair color, and other traits from our biological parents. That's why we look the way we do."

Rather than try to smooth over differences and strike a color-blind attitude, acknowledge the differences within your family, and let your child know that you love the way she looks.

13. "Why couldn't someone teach my birth mommy how to be a mommy?"

"Some women are not ready to be mommies, and they want their child to be with another mommy who is ready. Your birth mommy was wise enough to know that she was not ready to be a mom, so she made the decision to have someone else raise you."

14. "If you were my birth mother, would you have kept me?"

"Wow, that is a big question.... Your birth mom had to make a very difficult decision that I will never have to make. You are my son and we are a family, and nothing will ever change that."

15. "Do I have any brothers or sisters?"

"You have birth siblings. When you were born, your birth mother had two older boys. Those boys were in school and could take care of some things for themselves, but a baby needs much more care. Your birth mom knew she couldn't care for a baby at that time in her life, so she made a plan to find a family who would be able to take care of you forever." If you don't know, say so: "I don't know, but you might have birth siblings. Many birth parents have other children, born either before or after making an adoption plan."

16. "Now that Ellen is married, will I go back to live with her?"

"No. I know that, when we've talked about adoption before, I said that Ellen made an adoption plan for you because she was young and didn't have anyone to help her take care of a baby. But when we adopted you, we became your family forever. Dad and I will always be your parents, even when you're a grownup."

You might show your child her adoption decree or a photo taken the day her adoption was finalized in court.

17. "Why is Ellen going to be this baby's mommy but not mine?"

"It must hurt to think about your birth mom raising other children. Sometimes families go through hard times. It wasn't anything you did wrong. When you were born, Ellen didn't have anyone to help her and couldn't take care of you. You couldn't wait until later. You needed a safe family to help you grow up. Now Ellen is able to be this baby's mommy." [Or, if your child has older birth siblings] "When you were born, Ellen was just able to provide for her other children, but she knew that there wasn't enough food for one more baby. She wanted you to have a forever family to take good care of you."

18. "Why won't this baby be my baby sister?" [If an adoption match falls through]

"In order for a family to adopt a baby, the birth mother has to decide that she isn't able or ready to be a mommy. Your birth mother felt that way, and that's why we adopted you and we're your forever family. This baby's mother decided that she was ready to be a mommy, so the baby doesn't need to be adopted. We will wait for another baby to be your baby brother or sister."

19. "Did my birth parents love each other?"

"From what I understand, your birth parents were young and just beginning to explore relationships with the opposite sex. Sometimes young people become physically intimate when they're really seeking emotional closeness. I don't think they were involved long enough to develop that kind of closeness."

20. "My real mom would let me stay out past midnight!"

"Right now, we're not talking about my being 'real' or 'unreal,' we're talking about the fact that we're not going to make your curfew any later. We can talk about my reality as a parent another time."

A day or two later, you can say, "Remember when you were upset about your curfew the other day? I know you were angry with me when you implied that I'm not your 'real' mother. Now that we've calmed down, I am wondering if there's a question you'd like to ask me about your birth parents, or something you want to talk about. I know you think about them. What can I help you with?"

https://www.adoptivefamilies.com/talking-about-adoption/questions-about-adoption-kids/

APPENDIX 2

Thirty Things Adolescent Adoptees Wish They Knew About Their Birthparents –But Often Are Afraid To Ask

By Laurie Elliott

Questions adolescent adoptees have about their birthparents.

Through working as a court-appointed agent with adoptees in search, I have learned that many older adoptees have nagging questions about their adoptions. They lacked some very basic information about themselves during their growing years, and this lack affected their sense of identity.

To help other adoptees avoid the same adoption-related identity issues, I made a list of the things that the adoptees I worked with most wanted to know about themselves, their birth parents, and their adoption circumstances. I recommend that adoptive parents try to gather as many answers to these questions as they can when their children are young and the information is easier to find.

I have been busy gathering information to share with my own nine children, and it has offered them a piece of who they are.

I also encourage parents to share this information with their child before adolescence to promote a stronger sense of identity and to avoid issues later on. Information that would be matter-of-fact to children at a young age becomes a crisis if they're older and don't know.

1. What are my birth parents' first and middle names?
2. Where was a born (hospital and city)?
3. What time was I born?
4. Were there any complications at the time of my birth?
5. Did my birth mother see me or hold me?
6. Who else was present at my birth?
7. What were the circumstances surrounding my placement?
8. Did my birth mother pick my adoptive family?
9. Did my birth mother know anything about my adoptive family? (Did she meet my adoptive parents?)
10. What did my birth mother name me?
11. Does anyone else in my birth mother's family know about me?
12. Who knows what?
13. How old were my birth parents when I was born?
14. Were my birth parents married when I was born?
15. Where did my birth parents go to high school? College?
16. What kind of students were they?
17. What religious backgrounds do my birth parents have?
18. What is my ethnic/racial background?
19. Did my birth parents marry each other or anyone else after I was born? Do I have any biological siblings? Do they know about me?
20. Did I go to a foster home after leaving the hospital?

21. What was my foster family's name? How long was I there?
22. What do my birth mother and birth father look like? May I have a picture of them? Are my birth parents still alive?
23. Do my birth parents love me?
24. Do my birth parents think about me? Did they ever regret their decisions?
25. Do my birth parents have any special talents, hobbies, or interests?
26. What traits did I inherit from my birth parents? Personality? Looks? Talents?
27. Did my birth parents write to me over the years (journal/letters in a file)?
28. Are there any medical concerns I should know about?
29. If I called my birth parents or wanted to meet them someday, what would they do?
30. What should I call my birth parents?

© Copyright Laurie Elliott 1996

First published in *Adoptive Families Magazine*, reprinted with permission of the author.

https://comeunity.com/adoption/realmoms/2teensask.html

APPENDIX 3

Thinking About Adoption: FAQs

By: Elaine Schulte, MD, MPH, FAAP

Choosing to adopt a child is a big decision and is a beautiful way to create or add to a family. Below you will find the answers to some commonly asked questions.

Q: I think I want to adopt. Where do I begin?

A: Thinking about adoption can be an exciting and overwhelming process, and with more than 125,000 children adopted in the United States each year, it's obviously become a popular option. *Adoptive Families* is an award-winning resource for parents-to-be navigating the adoption process and for parents raising children through adoption. Learn more about their How-to-Adopt and Adoption Parenting Network.

Q: What are the different types of adoption?

A: Children can be adopted through the national public child welfare system, private agencies, existing relationships, or the international process.

- In a **public adoption**, the child is placed in a home by an agency that is either operated by the state or contracted by the state. Public adoption requirements can vary by state.

- In a **private adoption**, placement is made by a nonprofit or for-private agency. Parents typically use an agency to assist with an international adoption.

- An **independent adoption** may be carried out by birth parents, a lawyer, a doctor, a religious leader, or any other person who can help connect a child with a family.

For private and independent adoptions, the birth parent(s) can decide whether or not he or she wishes to select the adoptive parents, meet with them, even maintain an ongoing relationship, if he or she so chooses. That is called an **open adoption**. In a **closed adoption**, the names of the birth mother and father and the adoptive parents are not shared with one another.

Q: What is the average cost of adopting a child?

A: The costs really depend on the type of adoption, and, to some extent, the length of time it takes to adopt. Costs can range from $0 to $50,000. Child Welfare Information Gateway has an excellent review of adoption costs with references. Many employers also offer adoption benefits to help offset the cost. In 2013 the Federal Adoption Tax Credit was created to help families cover the adoption costs, as well.

Q: How long does the process of adopting a child typically take?

A: Parents hoping to adopt need to be prepared for a long and bumpy ride. Again, the length of time varies based on the type of adoption. Adopting a newborn from the United States can sometimes be extremely quick and/or could take years. The length of time to adopt internationally also varies based on the country and the referral process. Adopting a child internationally who has special medical needs can happen within 2 to 3 years. Adopting a child from foster care may not take quite as long, but it can be more complicated.

Q: There are so many adoption agencies out there, how do I know which I should use?

A: Selecting an adoption agency requires patience and perseverance. It's important that prospective parents do their homework. This may start with an internet search. Parents should look for an experienced agency and make sure the agency's values align with their own. Agencies should be willing to share references. Talk to friends and colleagues about their experiences, as well.

Q: Where can I learn more about the laws governing adoption?

A: Information about adoption laws can be found on the Child Welfare Information Gateway, which is a service of the Children's Bureau in the U.S. Department of Health and Human Services.

Q: What sort of preparation do I need as a prospective adopting parent?

A: As you consider the type of adoption you are going to pursue, you will need to get ready to be an adoptive parent. There is no "one size fits all" preparation that provides exactly what you need. Many agencies offer pre-adoptive training for prospective parents. For children who are adopted from foster care, there may be mandatory certification or training. Talk to families who've already adopted and gone through the process. Familiarize yourself with all the legal, financial, medical, developmental, and behavioral issues related to adoption.

Q: How will I talk about adoption with my friends and family?

A: If nobody in your family or circle of friends has adopted a child, it can be difficult to broach the subject. There are a lot of misconceptions about the adoption process and adopted children in general, and talking about it will invite people to voice what they know. HealthyChildren.org's article, *Respectful Ways to Talk about Adoption: A List of Do's & Don'ts*, will help you learn the lingo, think about what you'd like to use, and educate your family and friends.

Q: What are the common medical and developmental concerns facing adopted children?

A: Many adopted children have unique medical, mental health and developmental needs that are rooted in their prenatal and pre-adoption histories. These needs may be present prior to, or at the time of adoption, or they may not appear for several to many years after adoption.

Additional Information from HealthyChildren.org:

- Respectful Ways to Talk about Adoption: A List of Do's & Don'ts
- Internationally Adopted Children: Important Information for Parents
- Inducing Lactation: Breastfeeding for Adoptive Moms
- When to Tell Your Child About Adoption

Elaine E. Schulte, MD, MPH, FAAP is a board-certified pediatrician and Professor of Pediatrics at the Cleveland Clinic Lerner College of Medicine at Case Western Reserve University. She is the Medical Director of the Adoption Program at Cleveland Clinic Children's and has cared for hundreds of families and children touched by adoption. She also provides pre-adoption consultation service through MyConsult. Within the American Academy of Pediatrics, Dr. Schulte sits on the Executive Committee of the Council on Foster Care, Adoption, and Kinship Care. She is the parent of two children adopted from China.

American Academy of Pediatrics (Copyright © 2017)

About the Authors

Noah and I decided to co-write a book on both adoption types. Noah had an open adoption. I had a closed adoption. He was as confused as I was dealing with my issues. I never met my birth Mom or her family. As of the writing of this book, neither has Noah. – Scot

Noah: I have three siblings, my adopted Mom, and my Dad. I currently live in Duluth, Minnesota and am completing a church internship. I graduated from Urbandale High School, Urbandale, Iowa in 2019. I love sports and connecting with other young people. I have participated in football, tennis, and baseball over the years. My favorite vacation was in Colorado where we hiked in the mountains.

Scot: I graduated from Urbandale High School in Urbandale, Iowa in 1978. I was in the Air Force active duty and the Iowa Army National Guard part-time. I worked in counseling, the mortgage industry, and the insurance industry. I am currently retired. I volunteer 2-3 days a week at a prevention company that deals with kids. I also volunteer at my church. Even though my boys are adults, I still talk to them weekly.

www.ingramcontent.com/pod-product-compliance
Ingram Content Group UK Ltd.
Pitfield, Milton Keynes, MK11 3LW, UK
UKHW022222230426
12048UKWH00016BA/1011